Travel Through Time
War Machines

Military Vehicles Past and Present

Jane Shuter

Raintree
Chicago, Illinois

For more information address the publisher:
Raintree, 100 N. LaSalle, Suite 1200, Chicago IL 60602

Printed and bound in China by the South China Printing Company.

08 07 06 05 04
10 9 8 7 6 5 4 3 2 1

Library of Congress Cataloging-in-Publication Data:

Shuter, Jane.
  War machines : military vehicles past and present / Jane Shuter.
     p. cm. -- (Travel through time)
Includes bibliographical references and index.
Contents: Fighting machines -- War chariots -- Early warships -- Cannons at sea -- Life on a Man-of-War -- Tanks -- Submarines -- Early fighter planes -- Transport -- All at sea -- Second World War planes -- Planes since 1945 -- Modern wars.
  ISBN 1-4109-0583-7 (hc) 1-4109-0982-4 (pb)
  1. Transportation, Military--Juvenile literature. 2. Vehicles, Military--Juvenile literature. [1. Vehicles, Military. 2. Transportation--History.] I. Title. II. Series: Shuter, Jane. Travel through time.
UC270.S58 2004
623.7'4--dc21

2003010192

Acknowledgments
The publishers would like to thank the following for permission to reproduce photographs: p. 4 Werner Forman; pp. 5, 17, 21, 27, 28 Defence Picture Library; pp. 6, 7 Michael Holford; p. 8 Ancient Art and Architecture Collection; pp. 9, 10, 11, 14, 19 Peter Newark's Military Photos; p. 12 National Maritime Museum Greenwich; p. 13 Topham Picturepoint; p. 15 ATM Images; pp. 16, 20, 22, 23, 24, 26 Hulton Archive; pp. 25, 29 Corbis.

Cover photograph of an image of World War II reproduced with permission of Art Archive.

Every effort has been made to contact copyright holders of any material reproduced in this book. Any omissions will be rectified in subsequent printings if notice is given to the publishers.

Contents

Any words appearing in bold, **like this,** are explained in the Glossary.

Fighting Machines

Different groups of people have fought each other since the earliest times. Being able to move farther and faster than the enemy makes an army more likely to win. **Chariots** were first used in battle over 4,000 years ago. Since then, armies have tried to **invent** faster and more deadly vehicles.

In ancient times soldiers rode horses into battle, sometimes firing arrows at the enemy.

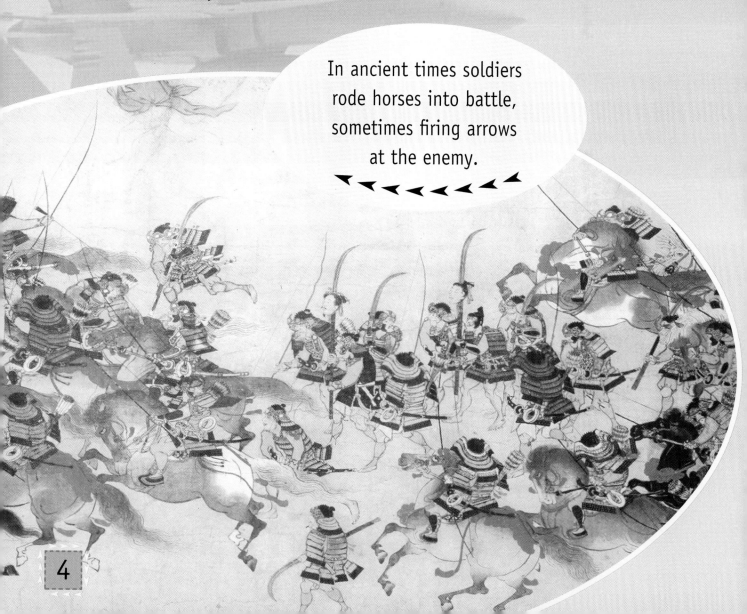

Soldiers wear **armor,** which covers their bodies with a hard surface. This makes it harder to injure them. Vehicles are also covered in armor. Too much armor makes a vehicle slow and difficult to drive. Vehicles and people need enough armor to be safe, but not so much that they cannot move around easily.

There is no-one on board this unmanned military vehicle (UVA). The **pilot** controls it from a safe place.

SAFEST OF ALL

Early armies fought hand-to-hand. By the early 1900s people could fight from vehicles that protected them. Modern armies often fight from a distance. Powerful **weapons** can be fired many hundreds of miles by a soldier who is safe in a hidden control room.

War Chariots

The first military vehicles were Sumerian war chariots, pulled by horses. Sumer was a country located in modern day Iraq. The Sumerians are the first people we know of that used the wheel. They used their chariots to carry equipment, as well as in battle. Without air-filled tires to protect them, the road surface would have been very bumpy.

This Sumerian box was made in about 2500 B.C.E. It shows their war chariots.

Safer than on foot?

As time passed people wanted to make war chariots faster and easier to turn and move. The best way to do this was to make the chariot smaller and lighter. They cut down the sides of the chariot, and used wheels that were not solid.

EGYPTIAN CHARIOTS

Ancient Egyptian war chariots were very light. This made them fast, but the driver had to be good at controlling the chariot and horses. The chariots easily overturned if they hit a rock.

This box shows the pharaoh Tutankhamen in his war chariot, fighting his enemies.

Early Warships

Early warships were built in various shapes and sizes. They were made to move fast, to **ram,** and to sink enemy ships. The earliest descriptions of sea battles are from the ancient Greeks. They talk of the sounds of splintering wood and screaming as ships rammed into each other and jammed together.

GREEK WARSHIPS

Greek warships had a heavy ram at the front of the ship. They were about 12 feet (3.5 meters) wide and 120 feet (36 meters) long. About 170 rowers were packed close together on three levels. These ships had no sails. Later warships had sails that they took down when they went into battle.

This is a modern model of an ancient Greek warship. When they overturned, very few rowers escaped.

Capture!

Starting around 1200 B.C.E. warships got bigger, heavier, and were powered by oars and sails. They cost a lot and took a long time to build. Sometimes sailors tried to board and capture enemy ships, not sink them. These warships, called **galleys,** would still rather ram and sink the enemy than lose the battle. These ships had fewer rowers than early warships. They carried more soldiers, including **archers** who fired arrows at the enemy from far away.

The Chinese were the first people to use **rudders** to steer their ships.

Cannons at Sea

The Chinese used **gunpowder** from about C.E. 1000, mainly in huge fireworks displays. It was not used much in sea battles until **cannons** were **invented** in about C.E. 1300. Cannons fired heavy iron cannonballs, which could easily make holes in the sides of a ship and sink it. Once cannons were invented, warships had to change.

The Battle of Lepanto in 1571 was the last big battle where galleys were used.

At first, cannons were just put on the decks of **galley** ships. Because of their weight, the cannon made ships harder to move. Sometimes the cannons bounced backward after firing cannonballs, which could overturn the ship.

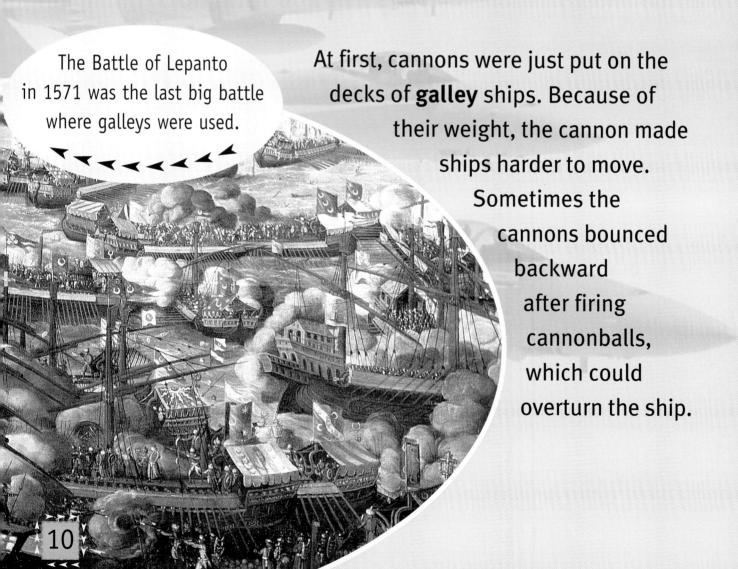

This painting shows British ships attacking Bunker Hill, Boston, in 1775, during the Revolutionary War.

A new design

One of the first warships built to carry cannons, the English *Mary Rose* was built between 1509 and 1510. It had cannons on deck and below deck, making the ship very heavy and hard to move around. By 1600, ships had more sails to use the wind to move faster and to change direction more easily. Ships armed with cannons attacked land as well as other ships at sea.

Life On a Man-Of-War

In the 1700s and 1800s fighting ships developed. There were several different sizes of ships. The biggest, a **first rate** man-of-war, could carry over 100 **cannons** and nearly 900 sailors. Life on board was hard for the sailors, even when they were not fighting battles.

This painting from the 1800s of life below decks shows things as far cleaner and less crowded than they really were.

OFFICERS AND MEN

The captain had his own **cabin** and dining room. The officers in charge of the ship shared a small room with bunks. The ordinary sailors slept in hammocks slung up over the cannons on the gun decks. They had no privacy at all.

Sailors got up at dawn, scrubbing the decks and cleaning the ship until 6 a.m. They had porridge for breakfast, and "Scotch coffee," a drink made from burned oatmeal and hot water. At midday they had salted meat, dried peas, and ships biscuits. These biscuits were made from flour and water with a pinch of salt, and were baked hard. For some sailors, the last meal of the day was porridge.

After a tough battle, sailors might gather together to pray for their wounded.

Submarines

Submarines are underwater warships that can creep up on the enemy without being seen. An early submarine was the *Hunley*, built in 1863 during the American Civil War. It moved just under the surface of the water, driven by eight men turning a pole joined to the **propeller.** The *Hunley* sank an enemy ship, the *Housatonic,* by **ramming** it under water with an explosive device. Unfortunately the *Hunley* also sank, maybe because the explosion made the water wavy and turned it over.

This is a photograph of the *Hunley* submarine. Once the sailors were inside they had no air and no light except a candle.

Modern submarines, such as this one, have large crews and lots of equipment.

NUCLEAR SUBMARINES

Nuclear submarines can stay under water for months, much longer than other submarines. They do not need to come up every few hours or days to get air as some others do.

Staying under

Submarines were used in World War I (1914–1918) and World War II (1939–1945). They were stronger and bigger than earlier submarines and could dive further and stay under water longer. The *Hunley* could stay under water for 25 minutes. By 1940 submarines stayed under for several hours or days. They fired torpedoes over longer distances. They had periscopes to look above the water, without coming up.

All at Sea

By 1900 fighting ships were made of metal and were bigger and heavier than men-of-war. They were not powered by rowing or using sails to catch the wind, but by steam engines. These battleships were much bigger and had more **weapons.** They, and their weapons, were expensive to make. If the enemy sank a battleship, it cost a lot to replace.

DESTROYERS

Destroyers were small, fast ships that traveled with large battleships, to keep them safe. They carried **torpedoes** to attack enemy ships.

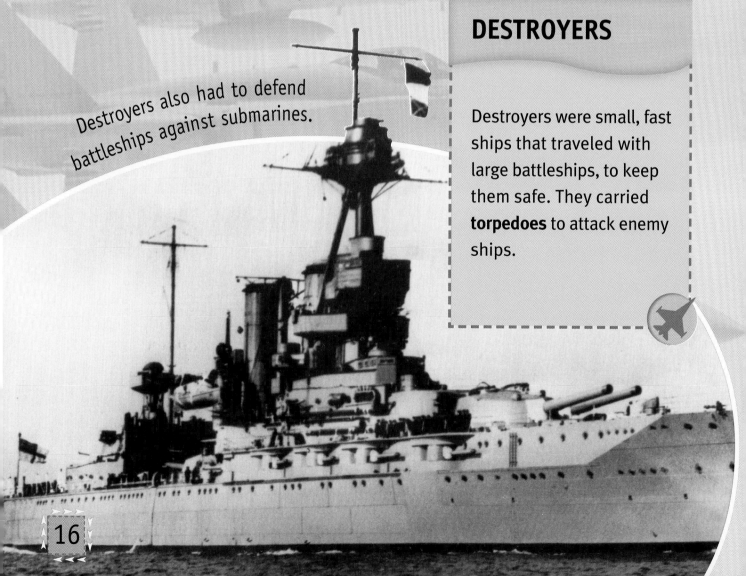

Destroyers also had to defend battleships against submarines.

Countries started to develop specialized landing craft, making it easier for soldiers to get to land.

In 1914 World War I began. Both sides began to make ships that were ready for war. Starting in 1910, long, flat decks were made on some ships, so planes could take off and land on them. These ships, called aircraft carriers, were not used in battle until close to the end of the war, in 1918. When **submarines** began to sink ships, **sonar** was developed. Sonar bounced sound waves off large objects underwater so submarines could be found and sunk.

Transport

All armies wanted fighting machines, but they also needed more ordinary military vehicles. They needed to move their soldiers and equipment around quickly. They also needed vehicles to get the wounded soldiers off the battlefield and into a hospital.

In the 1200s roads were so bad that it was easier for soldiers to move heavy supplies by sea.

Quick march

In early times armies used animals such as horses, oxen, and camels to carry their supplies or pull carts full of supplies. The army leaders rode horses, but ordinary soldiers marched.

As trucks, ships, and planes were **invented,** they were used to transport soldiers and their equipment. Sometimes special types of transport were **designed** for armies. One example is the aircraft carrier, a ship with a special runway for planes to take off and land.

JEEPS

Jeeps were first made for the United States army around 1940. They were called General Purpose Vehicles (GP for short). This became "jeep." Jeeps were small and quite light. They could easily speed across very bumpy ground.

This World War II jeep has just hit a very big bump.

Tanks

Tanks were big vehicles covered with **armor**, with a big gun on the top. Tanks were first used in World War I. They were very heavy, but had "tracks" to spread the weight and carry them over bumpy ground. The first time they were used in battle was by the British in 1916.

RIDING IN A TANK

Riding in a 1916 tank was hot and airless. The crew inside could only see out of the few air slits and holes for the **weapons.** The crew were thrown around inside the tank as it traveled over bumpy ground.

This early U.S. tank was photographed in 1917.

Better designs

Tanks have been used ever since 1916. Their **design** has been changed to make the ride less bumpy and to help the crew see more. Modern tanks also have radios to keep in touch with their base. Their armor plating keeps the crew safe from bullets. If they are hit by more powerful **ammunition,** such as bombs dropped from aircraft, it is hard for the crew to get out before the fuel tank explodes.

These modern tanks have been designed to fight in hot, sandy deserts.

Early Fighter Planes

The first **fighter planes** flew during World War I. There were big planes with a crew of up to eight, and planes for just one **pilot.** There were planes made of **canvas** and wood and others made of metal. Some planes had two wings on each side, others just one. All sorts of planes were open to the air, so the pilots and crew got very cold.

The Wright Brothers, who invented the airplane, made this first fighter plane for the U.S. army.

What were they used for?

Planes were first used for photographing enemy bases. Then pilots dropped bombs on the enemy. Pilots dropped the first bombs by hand, one by one. At first, pilots fought each other with handguns, then with guns fixed to the planes.

This photograph of Baron von Richthofen was taken in 1916.

THE RED BARON

One of the most famous fighter pilots of World War I was Baron von Richthofen, who shot down 80 British planes. He was nicknamed "The Red Baron" because he had his plane painted bright red. He was shot down on April 21, 1918.

Battles In the Skies

Planes played a big part in World War II. Some of the planes that were used were **fighters** and **bombers.** Fighter planes were small and light, with just the **pilot** on board. They flew at around 400 miles (643 kilometers) per hour. Fighters only had enough fuel to fly about 470 miles (757 kilometers). Bomber planes, with heavy bombs on board, were bigger, heavier, and slower. Some flew at around 220 miles (354 kilometers) per hour. They could fly about 1,500 miles (2,400 kilometers), though.

This B17 bomber plane was photographed in 1945.

Both sides bombed each other's cities and also soldiers, airbases, and ships. It was an air attack on the United States' fleet at Pearl Harbor, Hawaii, by the Japanese that pulled the United States into the war.

AIR INVENTIONS

New inventions could take time to be used, after they were first invented. They had to be tested for safety, and people trained to use them properly.

What?	Why?	First used
radar	to spot aircraft using radio waves	1936
jet engines	to go faster	1939
helicopters	to land in difficult places	1939

This photograph shows Japanese planes coming in to attack Pearl Harbor in 1941.

Planes Since 1945

Since 1945 fighting planes have changed a great deal. New technology has made them lighter, stronger, and faster. It has also made them more expensive. A World War II **bomber** would cost around $200,000 to build today. A modern bomber plane costs hundreds of millions of dollars to build.

HELICOPTERS

Helicopters have a large rotor blade on the top that spins around very fast to make them fly. They are useful in wars because they do not need a lot of space to take off and land. They have problems, though. They cannot carry much weight. They do not have a lot of space inside and they are very noisy.

These helicopters have just dropped US soldiers off in a jungle clearing.

The stealth bomber has a special coating on the outside, which makes it hard for enemy radar to spot.

Modern fighting planes have a lot of complicated equipment. Computer technology tracks other planes, finds out where the **pilots** are, and can even be set to fire **weapons** for them. Some armies are very close to having a working plane that can be flown almost anywhere in the world while the pilot controls it from somewhere else.

Modern Wars

Armies that can use the latest modern technology do not need to travel to fight. They can fire **missiles** over long distances that cause a lot damage to the enemy. They can strike at once, rather than having to transport soldiers and machines to another place to fight.

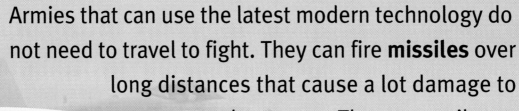

This is a U.S. Multiple Launched Rocket System (MLRS).

Computerized wars

Ships and other military vehicles are now worked by fewer people. Computers do much of the work that people once did. Scientists think that it will soon be possible to drive almost any vehicle by computer.

Wars are usually about taking over another country. Even if they begin fighting at a distance, soldiers have to go to the country they are taking over at some point. They have to go there to keep control. Then they will need ordinary military vehicles.

NOT ALL MODERN

Wars in small, developing countries do not have expensive, modern equipment. These armies still use older military equipment, including vehicles.

Even with all of today's modern technology, soldiers still need military vehicles such as tanks.

Find Out for Yourself

You can find out more about the history of military vehicles by talking to adults about how these vehicles have changed during their lifetimes. Your local library will have books about this. You will find the answers to many of your questions in this book, but you can also use other books and the Internet.

Books to read

Graham, Ian. *Designed For Success: Attack Fighters*. Chicago: Heinemann Library, 2003.

Oxlade, Chris. *Take off!: Transport around the world: Planes*. Chicago: Heinemann Library, 2001.

Using the Internet

Explore the Internet to find out more about military vehicles. Websites can change, but if the link below no longer works, don't worry. Use a search engine, such as www.yahooligans.com or www.internet4kids.com, and type in keywords such as "tank," "fighter plane," and "submarine."

Websites

http://www.army.mil/cmh-pg/

This website contains a wide assortment of books, documents, photos, and artwork documenting the history of the United States army.

Glossary

ammunition anything that is fired at the enemy to harm them

archer soldier who fires arrows from a bow

armor something that is used to protect soldiers or machines

bomber aircraft made to drop bombs

cabin room inside a vehicle

cannon large, heavy gun on wheels that fires large iron balls using gunpowder

canvas strong fabric

chariot platform on wheels, pulled by a horse or horses

design to plan, or decide how to make something

fighter plane aircraft made to fight with other aircraft

first rate a rating given to ships depending on their size. First rate ships were the biggest.

galley long, narrow ship powered by oars and sometimes sails, too

gunpowder mixture of chemical powders that explodes when lit

invent to make or discover something for the first time

missile anything that is thrown to hurt someone. Modern missiles have bombs fixed to them.

pilot person who flies a plane

propeller blade-shaped part of a ship or airplane that turns to make it move

ram to hit hard while going fast

rudder oar at the back of a ship that moves to change the direction of the ship

sonar when sound waves are bounced off large objects to locate them

submarine underwater ship

Sumerian person or object coming from the ancient country of Sumer, which is now modern Iraq

tank big vehicle covered with armor, with a big gun on the top

torpedo weapon fired from a distance under water

weapon object used for fighting

Index